1 & 2 Thessalonians

The Return of Jesus – Turning the World Upside Down

ISBN No: 1-905975-06-6

Published by Biblical Frameworks

Reg. Office: St Paul's Church, Robert Adam Street, London W10 3HW

Cover design, typesetting and production management by Verité CM Ltd, Worthing,
West Sussex UK +44 (0) 1903 241975

Illustrations by Richard Thomas

Printed in England

Biblical Frameworks is registered in England No: 5712581
Charity No: 1116805.

Contents

Book by Book

1 Introductory thoughts from Paul Blackham

The longest chapter in the Bible is all about… the Bible! Psalm 119 is all about the wonder of the Word of God. Verse 103 shows us the heart of someone who really loved the Bible. He cries out to the LORD God:

Psalm 119:103 – "How sweet are your words to my taste, sweeter than honey to my mouth!"

Whether you are reading the Bible alone or in some kind of group with others, expect to be thrilled by the words of the Living God. This is not like reading any other book. When we read and study the Bible the ultimate Author can be present with you, showing you His words and applying them to you.

Thousands of small groups are starting up all over the world – but what is it that is going to sustain them? It has to be the Bible.

So often, people don't quite know what to do with these small groups. Meeting together, sharing testimonies and experiences or sharing the odd verse is ultimately too sparse a diet to sustain people's spiritual needs in the long run, and really help them to grow.

What is needed is confidence in the Bible, and the ability to go to a *book* of the Bible rather than just an isolated verse. Each book of the Bible was written with a purpose, and it is only as we digest it as a book that we understand the real message, purpose, direction, storyline and characters.

It's a lot easier than people often think. You might think, "Oh, I can't manage a whole book of the Bible", but what we're trying to do in Book by Book is to break it down and show that it's easy.

The Bible was written not for specialists, not for academics – it was written for the regular believers, down the ages.

The world is in desperate need of answers. How can the world live at peace? How can we live together with justice and truth and compassion? There are so many religions and so much division and bloodshed: what is the real and living way that takes us to the Living God who can give us all a new beginning?

The Bible is the answer of the Living God to all our questions.

Our desire is that many Christians would experience the joy and confidence in the Scriptures that is found throughout Psalm 119 – "How sweet are your words to my taste, sweeter than honey to my mouth!"

2 All about Book by Book

A. WHAT IS BOOK BY BOOK?

Book by Book is a Bible Study resource with accompanying DVD. It has been designed principally for use in small groups, but can also be used for personal study or larger group situations.

B. THE STRUCTURE OF BOOK BY BOOK:

The Study Guide

The Study Guide provides the following features for each section of study:

- A Key Truth to focus on the most important truth in that section of the Bible Book.

- A Mind-Map diagram giving an overview of the study.

- An explanation of the Bible text, divided under suitable headings.

- Further Questions, to stimulate deeper thought and discussion.

- A week of suggested daily Bible readings to fill out and explore the themes from the study.

- A Bible Study, with detailed questions, designed to lead the individual or group deeper into the text.

A Bible Study answers section at the back of the study guide, for extra help if you need.

The DVD

Key features provided on each DVD are as follows:

- There is a 15 minute discussion on the DVD linked to each section of the Study Guide Bible passage
- The on-screen host is Richard Bewes, with co-host Paul Blackham. A specially invited guest joins them in the Bible discussions.

C. SOME TIPS ON HOW TO USE BOOK BY BOOK

The beauty of Book by Book is that it offers not only great Biblical depth, but also flexibility of approach to study. Whether you are preparing to lead a small group, or study alone you will find many options open to you.

And it doesn't matter if you are a new Christian or more experienced at leading Bible studies: Book by Book can be adapted to your situation. You don't need to be a specially trained leader.

Group study: preparing

- Select your study (preferably in the order of the book!)
- Watch the DVD programmes
- Read the commentary
- Use the suggested Bible questions…
- …or formulate your own questions (the mind maps and key truths are a great guide for question structure)

Group study: suggested session structure

We recommend you set aside about an hour for each study

- 5 minutes – read the relevant section of the Bible

- 15 minutes – watch the DVD programme

- 30 minutes – work through the Bible study questions (either your own or the ones in the guide), allowing time for discussion

- 10 minutes – If the study got the group thinking about wider issues of life today, then consider the Further Questions to stimulate a broader discussion

- Taking it further – suggest that group members look at some of the Daily Readings to follow up on the theme of the study

Given the volume of material you may even choose to take two weeks per study – using the DVD to generate discussion for one week and the Bible Study questions for the next.

Individual study:

There is no set way to conduct a study – here are some ideas:

- Select your study (preferably in the order of the book!)

- Read the Bible passage and related commentary.

- Try looking at the Mind-Map diagrams and seeing how the book has a structure.

- Take a look at the Key Truths and decide if they are the same conclusions you had reached when you read the book.

- Perhaps focus on the week of daily Bible reading to help you to explore the rest of the Bible's teaching on the themes of each section of study.

- Work through the Bible Questions. Don't worry if you get stuck, there is an 'answers' section at the back of the Guide!

Bookby**Book**

Overview of 1 & 2 Thessalonians

1 & 2 Thessalonians - The Return of Jesus - Turning the World Upside Down

1. What are you waiting for?
   1 Thessalonians. 1:1-10

   a. Paul and Silas at Thessalonica [Acts 17:1-9]
   b. Giving Thanks [1 Thessalonians 1:1-5]
   c. Imitating Paul [1 Thessalonians 1:6-8]
   d. Turning from Idols [1 Thessalonians 1:9-10]

2. Who are you trying to please?
   1 Thessalonians. 2:1-16

   a. Pleasing God, not men [1 Thessalonians 2:1-12]
   b. The Word of God, not men [1 Thessalonians 2:13-16]

3. How are you going to live?
   1 Thessalonians. 2:17-4:12

   a. Glorying in them [1 Thessalonians 2:17-20]
   b. Fearing for them [1 Thessalonians 3:1-5]
   c. Encouraged by them [1 Thessalonians 3:6-10]
   d. Praying for them [1 Thessalonians 3:11-12]
   e. Control our own bodies [1 Thessalonians 4:1-8]
   f. Love one another [1 Thessalonians 4:9-12]

4. What does the future hold for you?
   1 Thessalonians 4:13-5:28

   a. Encourage one another [1 Thessalonians 4:13-18]
   b. Times and Dates [1 Thessalonians 5:1-3]
   c. Night and Day [1 Thessalonians 5:4-11]
   d. Through and Through [1 Thessalonians 5:12-28]

5. When will our suffering end?
   When will there be justice?
   2 Thessalonians 1:1-2:12

   a. Growing under Pressure [2 Thessalonians 1:1-3]
   b. Pay back Time [2 Thessalonians 1:4-12]
   c. Rebellion and Lawlessness [2 Thessalonians 2:1-12]

6. How are you going to wait?
   2 Thessalonians 2:13-3:17

   a. Sharing the glory of Jesus [2 Thessalonians 2:13-17]
   b. Protected and Obedient [2 Thessalonians 3:1-5]
   c. Busy and Productive Lives [2 Thessalonians 3:6-12]
   d. Family Discipline [2 Thessalonians 3:14-18]

Study 1   What are you waiting for?

1 THESSALONIANS 1:1-10

> **Key Truth:** The heart of the Christian life in this passing age is waiting for Jesus to return to earth from heaven.

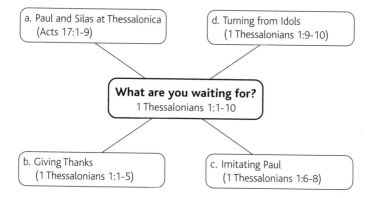

a. Paul and Silas at Thessalonica (Acts 17:1-9)

d. Turning from Idols (1 Thessalonians 1:9-10)

What are you waiting for?
1 Thessalonians 1:1-10

b. Giving Thanks (1 Thessalonians 1:1-5)

c. Imitating Paul (1 Thessalonians 1:6-8)

a.   Paul and Silas at Thessalonica (Acts 17:1-9)

1 Thessalonians is a letter written not just from Paul, but also from Silvanus (Silas) and Timothy – and when we remember what happened in Acts 17 we see why. From Philippi Paul & Silas went to Thessalonica, and Paul began teaching in a synagogue for three Sabbaths (Acts 17:2). Their time at Philippi had been dramatic, including a miraculous jail break. Nevertheless the Philippian church had been wonderfully established and even in the month that Paul was at Thessalonica he was surprised to receive more than one parcel of money from the Philippians (Philippians 4:16).

In Thessalonica Paul pointed out what the Scriptures taught about the Messiah (His suffering, death and resurrection), then he showed that Jesus is the one that the Scriptures were speaking of. This message had a great impact on the Gentiles as well as some Jews, but the trouble from Philippi had followed them.

Gathering a mob some unbelieving Jews attacked Jason's house where Paul & Silas were staying. These "unpersuaded" Jews were motivated by envy, seeing that Paul had won so many people to the truth of the Scriptures concerning Jesus the Messiah. Jason and his family were dragged to the authorities who were told: "These men who have turned the world upside down have come here also…" (New King James version).

It seems that Paul had particularly spoken about the coming Kingdom of King Jesus, because the sinful Jews and their mob accused Paul of announcing an alternative earthly ruler to Caesar. This feature of Paul's teaching sets the agenda for the two letters to the Thessalonians – *the date and nature of the return of King Jesus.*

It is quite true that the news of Jesus *did* turn the world upside down, because it showed that Caesar was simply a little, temporary ruler under the ultimate authority of Jesus. However, the unbelieving Jews were quite wrong to portray Jesus as simply one more earthly ruler alongside all the others. His Coming Kingdom is utterly different to the kingdoms of this world, and the Thessalonian letters show this very clearly.

These anti-Messiah Jews caused such trouble that the new Christians had to send Paul & Silas away to Berea, where they received a much better reception. Leaving Silas & Timothy in Berea, Paul went to Athens. Silas & Timothy must have rejoined Paul in Athens, because in 1 Thessalonians 3:1-2 Paul writes that he was so concerned about leaving the Thessalonian Christians in that situation of persecution, that he sent Timothy from Athens to encourage them. It must have deeply troubled Paul that these brand new believers were suffering such severe persecution so soon. Would they simply be driven out, imprisoned or killed by the Thessalonian anti-Jesus Jews? Would they become victims of the unbelieving Jewish heresies, turning them away from trusting in Jesus? The Galatian church was almost destroyed by the anti-gospel heresies taught by those who rejected Jesus.

Timothy returned to Paul with excellent news (1 Thessalonians 3:6) at Corinth (Acts 18:5). The young Thessalonian church was not only surviving but flourishing. The first letter to the Thessalonians seems to have been written while Paul was at Corinth with Timothy & Silas, because Paul writes in 1 Thess 2:17 that he had only been away from them for a short time.

Soon after that first letter arrived at Thessalonica it seems that a *false* letter arrived. We can see this in Paul's repeated references to letters in 2 Thessalonians (2 Thessalonians 2:2, 15; 3:14, 17). This false letter most likely claimed that King Jesus had already returned. The Thessalonians were very excited about the return of Jesus and this letter seems to have caused quite an impact in their fellowship (2 Thess. 3:11-12). Paul had to correct this error urgently.

It seems likely that Paul wrote his second letter while he was still at Corinth because it is also written in the company of Timothy and Silas. He expects them to still remember all that he told them on his visit (2 Thess. 2:5). Yet, enough time had passed for him to praise them on their continued growth and faithfulness (2 Thess. 1:3-4).

Timeline for 1 & 2 Thessalonians

1. Paul & Silas leave Philippi. (possibly Timothy is with them...but if not, he meets them at Berea - Acts 17:14). *(Acts 16:40)*

2. Paul & Silas on a 1 month mission in Thessalonica. They presumably intended to stay longer because they began working to earn money. *(Acts 17:1-9)*

3. Paul & Silas had to go to Berea, where Timothy is also mentioned. *(Acts 17:10-14)*

4. Mob force Paul to go to Athens, leaving Silas & Timothy. *(Acts 17:15)*

5. Paul commands Silas & Timothy to join him. *(Acts 17:15)*

6. While Paul is waiting for them, he preaches to the Athenians. *(Acts 17:16-32)*

7. Paul sent Timothy to Thessalonica from Athens. *(1 Thessalonians 3:1-2)*

8. Paul went to Corinth *(Acts 18:1)*

9. Paul preached the gospel in the synagogue every Sabbath. *(Acts 18:2-4)*

10. Silas & Timothy rejoin Paul at Corinth with news from Macedonia (Acts 18:5), especially Thessalonica *(1 Thessalonians 3:6).*

11. This news prompted the Spirit to drive Paul into new evangelistic zeal *(Acts 18:5).*

12. Paul stayed a long time in Corinth *(Acts 18:18)*. While he was at Corinth it seems most likely that he wrote the 3 letters: *Galatians, 1 Thessalonians and 2 Thessalonians.*

b. Giving Thanks (1 Thessalonians 1:1-5)

In addressing this first letter Paul indicates that the Thessalonian church is flanked by God the Father on one side and the LORD Jesus Christ on the other (verse 1). They are never alone no matter how much opposition they receive. The fact that Paul so naturally refers to Jesus as *the LORD* indicates that the deity of Jesus was not a difficult problem for him to struggle with, but a wonderful truth that he had shared with them from the Scriptures while he had been at Thessalonica.

Every day Paul thanked God for the faithful stand of the Thessalonian church (verse 2). They were full of faith, love and hope. Their trust of the Father and the Son, their love for each other and the world, and their great hope of Jesus' return kept them working at their witness, even though they had so many reasons to be disheartened.

This genuine spiritual fruit was the proof that the Thessalonian church was 'chosen' (verse 4). They were not a mere human institution, but an authentic part of the chosen Bride of Christ. This had already been shown in the way that the Holy Spirit had been so obviously at work when Paul and Silas had been preaching there. Their words were not mere human words, but words that were spoken in the power of the Spirit convincing the Thessalonians of their truthfulness.

We need to remember this as we speak about Jesus, explaining the Bible. If we were speaking our own ideas then we would have to rely on our own power and persuasion. However, if we are faithful to the gospel of God, then our words carry great power and authority. The Spirit Himself is at work within those we speak to, convicting them about Jesus. We might feel that those we are speaking to are hopelessly closed to the gospel, but we must remember that we are ambassadors of the mighty Holy Spirit who can open blind eyes, liberate closed minds and break the hardest hearts.

c. Imitating Paul (1 Thessalonians 1:6-8)

Paul & Silas were not only speaking powerful words at the Thessalonians. They *lived out* those words for everybody to see (verse 5-6). Paul will explain this in much more detail in chapter 2.

The message of this letter is about being faithful through opposition. This was exemplified by the apostles and, definitively, by Jesus Himself. The Thessalonians imitated this as they joyfully welcomed the gospel regardless of the fierce opposition they faced.

Their joy was from the Holy Spirit, according to verse 6. Sometimes Christians want to experience the great joy of the Spirit in the middle of a comfortable and easy situation. That is not normally how the Spirit works. His great passion is the gospel of Jesus, and it is as we are involved in that faithful and sacrificial witness that we find ourselves experiencing the intimate fellowship of the Spirit.

We know the joy of the Spirit as we join Him on the front-line of Christian witness.

The Thessalonians stood firm under opposition, and this became an encouraging, inspiring model for all the other churches in the region (verse 7). In fact, it was such a good example of following Jesus and His apostles that it had become a "world news item" (verse 8).

The force of verse 8 is lost in some English translations. The New King James version puts it well: "For from you the word of the Lord has sounded forth, not only in Macedonia and Achaia, but also in every place. Your faith toward God has gone out, so that we do not need to say anything."

It is good to see that such new Christians were already sending out evangelistic teams to the surrounding area. The example and proclamation of the Thessalonians was so striking and so well known that Paul, Silas and Timothy didn't need to say anything at all! The Thessalonian church had put *JESUS* on the front page of all the newspapers in the region. The chat must have asked the question "how could these Thessalonian citizens stand firm for the Jewish Messiah when there was so much public opposition to the message?!" Jesus was being discussed in the editorials and letter pages.

Standing firm against the world, the flesh and the devil is not just for our own personal benefit. When we see how other Christians endure great temptation and persecution, or the way a believer maintains a consistent evangelistic witness in their neighbourhood or workplace, we are strengthened in our own situation. Supporting churches under persecution not only helps the suffering Christians, it refreshes us to follow their example.

d. Turning from Idols (1 Thessalonians 1:9-10)

The chapter ends with one of the great definitions of what it means to follow Jesus. If we set out verses 9-10 we can see what Paul is saying.

You turned to God from idols –

- to *serve* the Living and True God &
- to *wait* for His Son from heaven (whom He raised from the dead), JESUS, who rescues us from the coming wrath.

"You turned to God from idols". In Acts 17:1-9 Luke does not describe Thessalonica as a city characterised by idolatry, as he does for Athens in 17:16. So, why does Paul speak of the Thessalonians turning from idols? Idolatry is much deeper and wider than bowing down to man-made statues of gods. In Ephesians 5:5 Paul writes that greed is idol-worship.

When we desire all the *things* that other people possess we are worshipping the creatures rather than the Creator. Jesus taught that the basic choice in life is between God and money (Matthew 6:24). The fundamental shift that the gospel of Jesus brought to the Thessalonians was a turning away from idolatry to the Living God.

"...to *serve* the Living and True God". Following Jesus is turning *from* idolatry, but turning *towards* a new life of serving the everlasting Father – from a life of pointless, empty pursuits towards a life of eternal purpose and significance. In this letter Paul is going to teach us what a Christian life really looks like, but here he summarises it all as "serving the Living and True God." We have a great dignity in this. No matter how little status we are given by the world around us, yet we are valued emissaries of the Living God. Every Christian really is "on a mission from God".

"...to wait for His Son from heaven." Throughout this letter Paul will always keep the return of Jesus in our vision. The key to turning from idolatry and serving God lies in waiting patiently and confidently for the return of Jesus. We can turn away from our greed, selfish ambition and evil desires only as we see the glorious future that is guaranteed in Jesus.

This is why Paul concludes with two statements about the future.

First, the Father raised Jesus from the dead. Therefore we can face our own death with peace and hope. If the Thessalonian Christians even had to die for Jesus they knew that their bodies would be restored as soon as Jesus returned.

Second, the return of Jesus is the day of His wrath. When He returns He will judge the whole world and all those who have not trusted in Him will face the terror of His wrath. However, He will rescue us from that wrath if we turn to Him now. We need not seek revenge or repay evil with evil when we suffer for Jesus because judgement belongs to Jesus.

If the Thessalonians fixed their hopes clearly and faithfully on their wonderful resurrection future with Jesus then they would be able to endure the lies, violence, rejection and pressure of witnessing to Jesus in Thessalonica. It is not enough to grit your teeth and exercise will-power to stand faithfully through such suffering. Jesus Himself endured the Cross *for the joy that was in front of Him* (Hebrews 12:2).

We can only follow Him through the Cross if we follow His certain hope of resurrection and glory.

The arrival of Jesus from heaven is mentioned at the end of each chapter in this little book, showing us that it is the heart-beat of Paul to the Thessalonians (1:10; 2:29; 3:13; 4:17; 5:23).

Study 1   Bible Questions

1 Thessalonians 1:2-10

1. In verse 3, what are the motivations for how the Thessalonians live and work?

2. Think about what inspires you to take action. How can we ensure our own motivations are the same as these?

3. How do verses 2-3 help us to pray for our fellow believers?

4. From verses 4-7, how does Paul know the Thessalonians are definitely Christians?

5. Read the account in Acts 17:1-9 of the founding of the Church in Thessalonica. Bearing this in mind whilst we study our passage, in what ways are the Thessalonians already a model to us as believers?

6. What do verses 8-10 tell us about the 'evangelistic strategies' of the Thessalonians and their effects?

7. Think about what people would say when they talk of our behaviour. Would it be anything like the accounts given of these young believers? As a group, how can we encourage one another to live out the gospel in our words and actions so that people will know that we live for Jesus?

Spend some time praying that you will be able to do these things in the coming weeks.

Study 1   Further Questions

1. Could we describe the society around us as an idol worshipping culture? What are the great idols of the modern world?

2. If our words about Jesus are backed by the power of the Spirit to convict our listeners, do we need to put effort into *presenting* our words? Is there a difference between 'trusting in techniques' and working to make our words clear and simple? Do we need to make our words persuasive and user-friendly if the Spirit is doing the convincing?

3. What kind of suffering do *we* face in speaking about Jesus? Is it possible to be faithful to Jesus and avoid all such suffering?

Study 1   Daily Readings

Day 1	Acts 17:1-9
Day 2	1 Thessalonians chapter 1
Day 3	Philippians 4:10-20
Day 4	Psalm 86
Day 5	Hebrews 11:1-16
Day 6	Matthew 10:1-20
Day 7	Matthew 10:21-42

The daily Bible readings are an opportunity to not only read through all of the material in the book under study, but also to read parts of the Bible that relate to the themes and issues that we have been considering. We try to make sure that we receive light from the whole Bible as we think through the key issues each week.

1 Thessalonians 2:1-16

> **Key Truth:** There will always be opposition to faithful gospel witness, but the reality of the gospel is clearly shown as we keep living and speaking the gospel.

```
          ┌──────────────────────────────────┐
          │   Who are you trying to please?   │
          │      1 Thessalonians 2:1-16       │
          └──────────────────────────────────┘
            ╱                              ╲
┌────────────────────────┐    ┌────────────────────────────┐
│ a. Pleasing God, not men │    │ b. The Word of God, not men │
│   (1 Thessalonians 2:1-12) │    │   (1 Thessalonians 2:13-16) │
└────────────────────────┘    └────────────────────────────┘
```

a.   Pleasing God, not men (1 Thessalonians 2:1-12)

Paul's mission to Thessalonica could easily look like a failure. After just three weeks there was such a city-wide rejection of the message of Jesus that there were riots in the streets. Paul & Silas had to be whisked away at night (Acts 17:10) to escape the trouble. Wasn't this a chapter in Paul's mission work that he would prefer not to mention?

Verse 1 – "You know brothers that our visit to you *was not a failure.*"

Paul explains his verdict (verse 2). They had been opposed at Philippi and must have felt the temptation to keep a low profile in Thessalonica. Surely they deserved a month of quiet preparation for the next campaign. Couldn't they be anonymous Christians for their stay in Thessalonica? NO! Paul says that the Spirit helped them to keep going, sharing the gospel "in spite of strong opposition". The fact that the gospel was proclaimed *against opposition* made it a success... because *that* is at the very heart of the way of Jesus.

Telling the gospel in spite of strong opposition showed the authenticity of the gospel itself. If Paul & Silas had been acting out of selfish motives then they would have simply kept quiet when things got too difficult. The fact that they kept on speaking about Jesus regardless of the opposition they faced showed the purity of their motives (verse 3-6). They were not speaking to get human approval, nor to get money out of anybody (verse 5). Rather, they spoke as men who were already approved by God, sent out to tell people about Jesus. Paul & Silas were more interested about God's testing of their hearts (verse 4) than the kinds of tests that we *humans* use to judge each other.

In verses 7-9 Paul explains how they behaved during their brief stay in Thessalonica. Paul was an apostle – a man who was personally commissioned by the Risen Jesus as one of the authoritative pioneers of the New Testament Church. The Holy Spirit enabled these twelve apostles to do many miraculous signs to demonstrate their apostolic authority.[1] Paul spoke and wrote with the very authority of the LORD Jesus Himself. Yet, when Paul & Silas came to Thessalonica Paul did not throw his weight around as a spiritual celebrity. He did not make himself the centre of attention, taking all the money and affection from devoted followers. No, Paul did not insist on the respect and support that he deserved as an apostle. Paul & Silas were not a burden to the Thessalonians, but instead cared for them with all the gentleness and self-sacrifice that we might see in a mother caring for her little children (verse 7).

Verse 8 is one of the golden verses of this letter. Paul & Silas loved the Thessalonians so much that they shared their lives with them, not just the gospel.

Sharing the gospel could not be done effectively from an impersonal distance. The apostles showed the authenticity of the gospel, of Jesus, through their generous, open lifestyle.

---

[1] See 2 Corinthians 12:12

The gospel is not a theory about the after-life, but a transformation of our lives beginning right here and now.

The reality of the gospel is seen as we share our lives with the people we are witnessing to. The truth of what we say is not demonstrated by the cleverness of our arguments.

The world is full of theories and arguments, but it is very rare to find a life that genuinely reflects the life of Jesus.

As we lay down our lives like Jesus, as we share His joy and hope, then we give people a real chance to see that the gospel is not human religion but the power of the Living God.

Paul and his friends worked hard to show that the news of Jesus was categorically different to anything that the Thessalonians knew (verse 9-12). Not only did they make sure they were generating their own funds for their work, but they treated those new believers just as a loving father would do to his own children. The Thessalonians perhaps expected philosophers or 'thinkers' to be trying to take money from people. It was crucial that Paul make no such demands. The time would come when they would have to pay their elders/ministers properly, but Paul wanted them to know that the planting of this church cost the Thessalonians nothing.

Verse 12 gives us the manner of Paul's teaching. He did not *command* or *order* these saints how to live. Paul had no hidden agendas of personal power. Like a gentle father, he *encouraged, comforted* and *urged*. He was alongside them in their first steps of spiritual growth.

In all this we see how Paul was working with his attention fixed only on the Father, Son and Holy Spirit. He was free – free from the demands, expectations, manipulations and motivations of those who want to win the approval of their own society and culture. It is this focus on Jesus that enables His servants to be such powerful forces in all the different situations of the world. The Church can offer a genuinely different way of life, a refreshing and holy explanation of the world. The Father is calling us into His kingdom and glory (verse 12) and as we give ourselves over to that calling, so we are set more and more free from the kingdoms and glory of this passing age.

b. The Word of God, not men (1 Thessalonians 2:13-16)

We saw in chapter 1 that the gospel preaching of Paul & Silas was empowered by the Holy Spirit. Paul was full of praise to God that the Thessalonians realised this and received their words as the very words of the Living God (verse 13).

This is one of the key marks of Christian life – receiving the words of the prophets and apostles as the very words of God. From the world's perspective Paul, John, Moses and king David were nothing more than human writers who expressed the religious thoughts, feelings and aspirations of their age and culture. We should continually praise God for the way the Spirit continually opens our sinful eyes to see reality – these words were breathed-out by God through these human writers. Our allegiance to the LORD is shown by our recognition of the teaching of the apostles as the word of God.

On another level it is important for us to remember that when we present the gospel message to those around us, our message is not our own. We are ambassadors entrusted with *God's* gospel. If we are faithful to that, then the issue is not whether people believe us but whether people will receive *Jesus*.

We can easily think that it is up to us to make this gospel message convincing… or even powerful. Yet, our essential job is to be faithful ambassadors (in words and actions) and leave it to the Living God to use His omnipotent power in His gospel work.

The proof that they had received the apostolic teaching as the word of God was the way the Thessalonians withstood the opposition of their fellow Thessalonians. Just as Jesus was rejected by His own people, so the Thessalonians had been granted the privilege of sharing in that same suffering with Jesus.

Why does Paul give such a stern warning here about those Jews who had turned away from their Scriptures and their Messiah? (verses 14-16).

Paul knew the terrible danger that they posed to these new Christians. Paul wrote his letter to the Galatians at this time and there we see just how deadly false teachers could be. In Galatia Jews had arrived who *trusted in the Law rather than Jesus the Messiah,* and they tried to get the Gentile believers to do the same.

In Thessalonica these unbelieving Jews had first tried to stamp out faith in the Messiah through physical violence and political oppression. When they saw that this would fail, their next strategy was to undermine the Thessalonians' faith in Jesus the Messiah. Paul was very worried that the Thessalonians might be deceived by these unbelieving Jews with their apparent love for the Scriptures. He had to let the Thessalonian church know that there have always been Jews who have opposed the LORD God of Israel and have misused the Scriptures to deflect people away from the Messiah. In fact, not only had they killed the prophets of Scripture but they actually killed Jesus the Prophesied Messiah (verse 15).

The Jewish people had more reasons to trust in Jesus than any other people in the world.[2] They had Abraham, Isaac and Jacob at the foundation of their nation, with all the Messianic promises given to them. They had the Law of Moses, which was a holistic, multimedia presentation of Messianic hope. They had the Messianic prophecies of David, Isaiah, Ezekiel, Jeremiah, Zechariah, Malachi and all the other prophets. *Jesus is a Jew.*

Many Jews did in fact believe in Jesus the Messiah (see Acts 2 for an example of 3,000 believing), but there were some who resolutely rejected all these testimonies to the Messiah. Not only did they personally reject Jesus, but they tried to prevent the message of Jesus

---

[2] See Romans 9:1-5

going out to the Gentile world. What happened in Acts 17 was not an isolated event, but a symptom of their rejection of the Jewish Messiah. This is why they provoked the anger of God to the extreme (verse 16).[3]

This warning from Paul was very wise, because when we study the second letter to the Thessalonians we do not find any of the problems that afflicted the Galatian church. The Thessalonians would be on their guard when unbelieving Jews tried to make them trust in the Law rather than Jesus.

Study 2   Bible Questions

1 Thessalonians 2:1-12

1. What effect has the gospel had on the lives of Paul, Silas and Timothy from verses 1-2? How and why did they continue to live in this way?

2. Why is gospel witness so often linked to suffering and persecution? (See 2 Timothy 3:12, 1 Peter 4:12-16)

3. Verses 3-6 are a real challenge to us. What should motivate us?

4. Why must our evangelism be free of error, trickery, flattery or greed? How can we share the gospel the way these men did, and avoid doing these things? Is it acceptable to draw people to an event without telling them that there will be a gospel message preached?

5. What else do we learn from verses 7-9 about how to share the gospel and carry out a godly ministry? How can we "share our lives" with others without neglecting our family life?

6. What does it mean to 'live lives worthy of God', verse 12? Explain how this does not mean we try to be 'good enough' for God. (1 Thessalonians 1:3)

---

[3] There is no violence in Paul's words. The evil of anti-Semitism can find no support from the Bible. Paul was ready to sacrifice his life and soul for his unbelieving Jewish brothers (Romans 9:3). Whether others believe in Jesus or not, the way of Jesus is the way of love and blessing, tolerance and self-sacrifice.

Study 2   Further Questions

1. How do we judge the 'success' of our evangelism? Is strong opposition a mark of success?

2. Are we excited by the thought of everybody in the world living like the Christians in our local church fellowship? In other words, can we see our local church fellowship as an answer to the world's problems?

3. Why did some of the Jews reject their prophesied Messiah? Were the Scriptures too vague or too complicated? Was Jesus different than the prophets predicted? Or was it simply wilful unbelief?

Study 2   Daily Readings

Day 1   1 Thessalonians 2:1-16

Day 2   1 Peter chapter 1

Day 3   James chapter 1

Day 4   Isaiah 49:1-7

Day 5   1 Samuel 16:1-13

Day 6   Acts chapter 2

Day 7   Psalm 139

The daily Bible readings are an opportunity to not only read through all of the material in the book under study, but also to read parts of the Bible that relate to the themes and issues that we have been considering. We try to make sure that we receive light from the whole Bible as we think through the key issues each week.

Study 3   How are you going to live?

1 Thessalonians 2:17-4:12

Key Truth: Focussing on the return of Jesus, and living according to His word is how we choose to live and bring glory to our King.

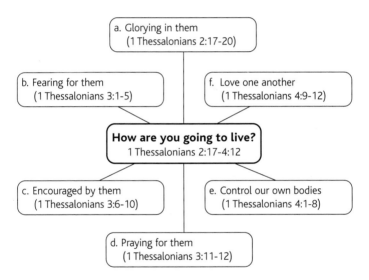

a.   Glorying in them (1 Thessalonians 2:17-20)

The Thessalonians were at the forefront of the gospel's expansion and Paul was very worried about them. These new-born saints needed encouragement and instruction if they were going to live out the gospel faithfully under so much pressure.

Paul longed to be with the Thessalonian Christians to help them through these difficult times. They were always on his mind. He constantly tried to return to them, but Satan kept preventing him.

This was a critical situation for Satan. He had enjoyed thousands of years of almost uninterrupted dominion over Europe. It seems unlikely that many Europeans joined the nation of Israel before the events of Pentecost. They were, as Paul puts it in Ephesians 2:12 "separate from Christ, excluded from citizenship in Israel and foreigners to the covenants of the promise, without hope and without God in the world."

With the globalisation of Israel at Pentecost a very much better future was coming to Europe.

Satan was fighting hard against it. If he could in some way destroy these early European churches then he might imagine that he could contain the outward rush of Israel. The Thessalonian church was at the top of Satan's agenda.

Paul agreed with Satan about the importance of the Thessalonians! However, whereas Satan hated these models of the power of the gospel, Paul loved them very deeply. He says that on resurrection morning, when Jesus returns, they will be his hope, joy and crown (verse 19). Evangelism is a way to secure eternal treasure. On Resurrection Morning we will be able to meet up with those people who learned about Jesus though our support and witness.

The Thessalonians were Paul's great proof that the gospel was the power of God for the salvation of everyone who believes in Jesus and that he was the apostle to the Gentiles. In fact, he didn't need to wait for the return of Jesus – they were the glory and joy of Paul, Silas and Timothy right there and then. In such a short time they had heard and responded to the liberating truth of the Divine Messiah and they were already living, functioning European citizens of Israel.

b. Fearing for them (1 Thessalonians 3:1-5)

With so much attention being focussed on the Thessalonians, Paul sent Timothy to see them as soon as he was able. In fact, Paul got Timothy moving so quickly Acts 17 doesn't even record Timothy arriving in Athens and being sent out again!

It was Timothy's job to strengthen and encourage the Thessalonians in their trust in Jesus. Paul commends Timothy as a partner in the gospel work, fully equipped to help them. Paul trusted that his apprentice knew how to strengthen this key church in this critical time. It is worth remembering the method that Paul instilled into Timothy.

> **1 Timothy 4:12-13** "Don't let anyone look down on you because you are young, but set an example for the believers in speech, in life, in love, in faith and in purity. Until I come, devote yourself to the public reading of Scripture, to preaching and to teaching."

> **2 Timothy 4:1-2** "In the presence of God and of Christ Jesus, who will judge the living and the dead, and in view of his appearing and his kingdom, I give you this charge: Preach the Word; be prepared in season and out of season; correct, rebuke and encourage – with great patience and careful instruction."

Paul's letters to Timothy surely reflect the method that Paul always taught Timothy. In order to be fruitful and faithful, Christian people do not need merely inspiring stories or stirring motivational speeches. No matter how much they worked on their image or improved community relations, Satan was determined to destroy them. The key to their survival was a constant feeding on the Scriptures, the Word of God. The mind of the Living God alone could give them understanding, love, confidence, hope and endurance.

For us today, whatever our cultural challenges, the Bible alone will make us both loving and truthful, accessible and radical, faithful and flexible.

Paul knew that it was not enough for Timothy to simply go and act as a "cheerleader" for the Thessalonians. In verse 3 he states that the trials they were all facing were destined for them. Their trials were not due to a mistake or sin they had done, or a flawed strategy they had pursued. Rather, persecution is an integral aspect of Christian living. Paul tells Timothy in 2 Timothy 3:12 – "everyone who wants to live a godly life in Christ Jesus will be persecuted..." It was vital that the Thessalonians understood this tough truth so that they would embrace their trials as a key aspect of their growth and discipleship. Satan will always try to make us think that we could have an easy, more fulfilled life if we just stopped following Jesus. It is no wonder that (verse 5) Paul was concerned for the Thessalonians.

The same lesson is crucial for us as well. It is always difficult to follow Jesus through the temptations and persecutions. Some of us face physical, even mortal, danger. Others of us face the constant temptation of materialism, popularity and self-indulgence.

Following Jesus is always very costly and unless we embrace that as an essential aspect of the Christian life we will fall under the pressure.

c. Encouraged by them (1 Thessalonians 3:6-10)

Paul's fears were relieved when Timothy reported back with such glowing accounts of the Thessalonians' faithfulness and growth. Perhaps Paul feared that in their sudden flight from the trouble at Thessalonica the young Christians might have felt abandoned and maybe even a little negative towards Paul & Silas. All these fears were unnecessary as they remembered them with affection and longed to see them (verse 6). Paul had shared his life with them, and they had responded with love.

On the one hand Paul wanted to encourage the Thessalonians in their trouble, but (verse 7) it was the news about the faithfulness of the Thessalonians that encouraged Paul, Silas and Timothy. When we are feeling the cost of following Jesus there is nothing so strengthening and inspiring as hearing about the steady faithfulness of others. When we keep on loving and following Jesus through thick and thin we are building up other Christians.

We should also remember that *unfaithfulness* is terribly discouraging to the Christian family. Imagine how devastated Paul would have been if the Thessalonians had gone back to their past ways of living and thinking. One of the most heart-breaking aspects of ministry is when a person pursues their selfish desires and forsakes Jesus. That individual tends to think only of their own situation, but their decision can cause spiritual disaster for other members of the Church family.

Verse 8 – "For now we really live, since you are standing firm in the faith. How can we thank God enough for you in return for all the joy we have in the presence of our God because of you?" Paul speaks almost as if his life were hanging in balance as long as he was unsure about the spiritual well-being of the Thessalonian church. What love and care he showed for that church! Far from them being a burden to Paul, Silas and Timothy, they couldn't stop thanking God for the joy they received from them (verse 9). This shows what they really wanted in life; what filled them with joy. Are we too filled with joy when we hear of the faithful witness of other Christians?

Paul couldn't wait to see them again and give them even more help (verse 10). If they had done so well when their knowledge of Jesus was so limited, how much better they would do when their faith was more developed!

d. Praying for them (1 Thessalonians 3:11-12)

It is always a great privilege when we are allowed to see the apostle Paul at prayer. So many of us wonder just how we are supposed to pray. When we listen in to Paul we are listening to a man whose prayer life was in real harmony with the will of God.

He has made it clear that Satan was working hard to prevent them going back to the Thessalonian church (1 Thessalonians 2:18).

They didn't use all their energy trying to outwit Satan. None of us are strong enough or clever enough to do that. Rather (verse 11) they put themselves completely in the hands of God the Father and God the Son. They *are* well able to clear Satan out of the way.

Now, what do we think the Thessalonian church needed most of all? Special protection from the Holy Spirit? Guardian angels? Better information? All these things would have been very useful, but in verse 12 Paul focuses on love. He wants the Lord Jesus to increase their love for each other and for everybody. Paul had experienced this overflowing love for them, and now he wants them to experience the same thing. Why? In their times of trouble they needed love for each other so very much. When the surrounding world hated them they could not afford to be fighting or being selfish towards each other.

The Christian family is our great strength and support in the hard times.

The conclusion of this short prayer begins to turn our attention towards the major theme of the letter: the return of Jesus. Paul's prayer is that the Thessalonians receive strength from Jesus so that they will turn away from sin and keep living holy lives right through to the end. They are to live with the return of Jesus constantly in their minds, because their lives are always "in the presence of our God and Father".

The world lives as if there is no God, no returning Jesus and no day of judgement. It is vital that we always live the truth: in the *presence* of God, *waiting* for Jesus and prepared for the final day.

e. Control our own bodies (1 Thessalonians 4:1-8)

As verse 1 tells us, Paul had told them how to live in expectation of Jesus' return and he was pleased to hear that they were doing this, but now he refreshes them on key features of this *holy waiting*. The future used to hold the pursuit of selfish desires followed by eternal damnation. Now a very different future lies before the Thessalonians, a future of dignity, freedom, holiness, love and joy, followed by a resurrection to immortality and everlasting life on the renewed earth!

The first item to address is the use of our bodies. If our hope includes the resurrection of our bodies, then the way we treat our bodies right *now* is very important. Our bodies are not "temporary shells" nor are we merely "naked apes". Rather, the LORD Jesus has given infinite dignity and honour to the human body through His birth, life, resurrection and future return. Paul seems to refer to the teaching of Jesus Himself in verse 2.

The will of God is that His people are holy (verses 3-4) – that is, that they are distinct from the unbelieving world in their service of God. The specific concern here (as so often in modern life) is sexual immorality.

The Bible often shows how sexual immorality springs from idolatry – and therefore sexual purity, both inside and outside of marriage, is a marvellous witness of true worship of the Living God.[4] As each Christian exercises *control* over their body, so they display holiness in contrast to the pagan abandonment to passionate lust. The pagan's ignorance of the Living God is shown in their inability to control their lusts.

This is very important teaching. Paul is aware that our sinful flesh is difficult to control because of our passionate lusts. The amazing gospel miracle is that our bodies do not have to be driven by such lusts. Living in the presence of the Father, strengthened by the Returning LORD Jesus and encouraged by the indwelling Holy Spirit the Christian can control their body (see verse 8).

This is not just for personal righteousness though. As Paul goes on to say in verse 6, the problem with uncontrolled lust is that it is an abuse of other people. It is very important that the Church is not a place where we take sexual advantage of each other. The LORD Jesus takes that abuse of our Christian fellowship very seriously indeed, and we should expect punishment for such sin (verse 6). Few things so

---

[4] See Leviticus 18:1-19:4. The laws concerning sexual relations begin and end with the affirmation that the LORD is the God of His people. Notice also verse 21. The worship of Molech and child sacrifice is addressed in the centre of the laws concerning sexual relations. Child sacrifice is associated with sexual immorality today just as then. Praise God that His free forgiveness and grace can deal with all our sins today just as then!

desperately undermine the gospel witness of the Church than sexual immorality. It is no surprise that Jesus is ready to act against it.

Verse 7-8 puts the matter with a refreshing clarity. Today people tend to react very strongly to anybody telling them how they should live. What right has any one of us got to tell someone else what is right and wrong? It is *not* mere human beings who have conjured up ideas about sexual morality and purity. It is our Holy Father God who has called His people to live a holy life… and in His Word He has told us just what He means by that. When "Christians" try to argue that it is ok to have sexual activity outside of the marriage of a man and a woman, it is important to remember that they are rebelling against the Father in heaven.

f.   Love one another (1 Thessalonians 4:9-12)

Paul's prayer had been for them to have an overflowing love for each other (3:12). Now it is time for him to drive that prayer home.

Paul begins with the wonderful fact that every new born, Spirit-filled person knows that we are to love each other (verse 9). Loving the Christian family is an essential identifying feature of salvation. No matter how much a person may talk about God or do 'Christian things', if they do not love the Christian family we must assume that they are not a genuine follower of Jesus. Paul (verse 10) wants them to love each other *more and more* – just as he had told them to please God in their lives *more and more* back in verse 1.

We can never love each other too much, never care for each other too much, never put too much time and energy into building each other up.

Verse 11 is a striking verse for us in the 21st century. Ambition reveals our hearts. What do we really want from life? What do we see as our purpose in life? If our ambition is to have plenty of money, fame, a beautiful home, professional acclaim or social status, then we show that our hope is fixed on earthly treasures that will pass away without trace. In Paul's seminar on Christian ambition we learn that our life's ambition must be *evangelism*, bringing unbelievers to Jesus.

We must not be troublemakers in our society nor must we be "drop-outs" making no contribution to the society. Christians must be *known* as good citizens, winning the respect of most people.

Paul further warns against interfering in other people's business (verse 11). One of the great temptations that the Christian can fall into is acting as a kind of moral policeman over other people, whether they are Christians or not. The only result of this is that people think that our message is "be good, don't do sinful things". In the modern western world it is all too common to find that people do not associate Christians with *following Jesus* but rather with campaigning for censorship, stricter drink/drugs laws and the imposition of "sexual restrictions", "prying into private bedrooms". It is not our job to make non-Christians behave as if they were Christians. Rather our ambition is for them to become Christians, to turn to Jesus away from their sin.

Paul's emphasis is not on pagans *behaving like* Christians, *but Christians really behaving like Christians*.

His instruction is for them to love each other more and more, to control their own bodies and to organise their lives so that the outsiders are drawn into the family of God.

Study 3   Bible Questions

1 Thessalonians 4:1-10

1. What have verses 1 & 2 to say to us when we are feeling lazy in our relationship with Jesus? Look also at 3:13 for our motivation.

2. What is the first way Paul mentions that we can live to please God, verse 3? What is the link between being holy and sexual purity? (See also Hosea 4:10, 5:4)

3. Why does Paul link sexual immorality with not knowing God (verse 5)? Whether we are married or single, what is the real marriage that we look forward to as Christians? Where do we find our completely satisfying intimacy? (Ephesians 5:31-32)

4. With this future reality in mind, how do you think the LORD looks on sexual immorality amongst His people? (1 Corinthians 6:12-17) Can you explain why the Bible relates it to idolatry? (1 Corinthians 6:18-20)

5. How would Paul counsel and comfort someone who had been involved in sexual immorality but now wanted to live a life of purity? (See also: 1 Corinthians 6:9-11)

6. Have you ever been laughed at or victimised for living or explaining your belief to be sexually pure? What comfort does verse 8 hold? Also what courage does it give us?

7. In what way had God taught the Thessalonians how to love each other, verse 9? (See 1 John 4:9-12)

8. From verse 10, haven't the Thessalonians loved their Christian brothers and sisters enough? Why do they have to continue in this, and what does this mean for us and the relationships within our church?

Study 3   Further Questions

1. What did Jesus mean when He told us to store up treasure in heaven? What is this treasure?

2. Why does the Bible show such deep respect for the human body? Why is such spiritual significance attached to our physical body, especially in terms of sexual practice?

3. Is it acceptable for Christians to be silent about Jesus when they are involved in social care and action? What is the Biblical connection between evangelism and social compassion?

Study 3   Daily Readings

Day 1	1 Thessalonians 2:17-4:12
Day 2	Acts 17:10-34
Day 3	Psalm 103
Day 4	1 Timothy chapter 4
Day 5	Genesis 2:18-25
Day 6	1 Corinthians 6:9-20
Day 7	1 John 4:7-21

The daily Bible readings are an opportunity to not only read through all of the material in the book under study, but also to read parts of the Bible that relate to the themes and issues that we have been considering. We try to make sure that we receive light from the whole Bible as we think through the key issues each week.

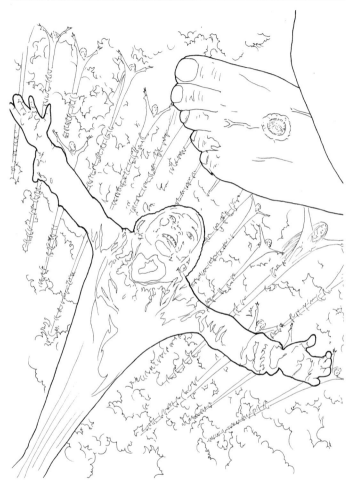

Caught up to meet Him

1 Thessalonians 4:13-5:28

> **Key Truth:** As Christians, we do not fear death, but eagerly await the return of Jesus, when all those who have trusted in Him down the ages will be united to Him and begin life on the renewed earth.

a. Encourage one another
   (1 Thessalonians 4:13-18)

d. Through and Through
   (1 Thessalonians 5:12-28)

What does the future hold for you?
1 Thessalonians 4:13-5:28

b. Times and Dates
   (1 Thessalonians 5:1-3)

c. Night and Day
   (1 Thessalonians 5:4-11)

a.   Encourage one another (1 Thessalonians 4:13-18)

Paul had clearly enthused the Thessalonians about the return of Jesus. We can only deny our evil desires and sacrifice our lives for the gospel if our vision is fixed on this glorious certainty in our future. As verse 18 says, we need to talk to each other often about the return of Jesus for our encouragement.

The Bible tells us so much about our resurrection future so that we can clearly, confidently anticipate it together.

However, the Thessalonians seem to have run up against a big problem.

Bookby**Book**

If Jesus is going to return *here*, to the earth, and live *here* forever after renewing the creation… well, what about those Christians who have already died and *gone away* from *here*?

If Christians have died and gone to heaven, then aren't they going to miss out on Jesus' return to earth?

Many modern Christians think so little about the return of Jesus that they think only of dying and going to heaven, but the Thessalonians were much closer to the Bible's teaching. They knew that the future is not about us going away to heaven, but Jesus returning to the earth.

Paul begins by making it clear that death is very different for the Christian (verse 13). We do not grieve as unbelievers who have no hope at all in the face of death. Rather, verse 14, the death and resurrection of Jesus proves to us that Christians who die will certainly not miss out on the resurrection future at the return of Jesus. *Jesus will bring them back with Him.*

Christians die and go to be with Jesus, but will join Him as He empties heaven on the Last Day.

Verse 15 is important. The Thessalonians have assumed that the Christians who are still on the earth when Jesus returns will be ahead of the dead Christians. Paul seems to go back to Jesus' own words concerning His return – see Matthew 13:41-43; 24:30-31. Jesus the Lord Himself will descend from heaven, in a very loud and public way, surrounded by His holy angels who will gather the wicked out of the world to be thrown into Hell.

His descending will be announced by three loud noises: His own word of command; the voice of the senior angel; and the great trumpet blast.

▪ Jesus spoke about His word of command in John 5:28-29 "Do not be amazed at this, for a time is coming when all who are in their graves will hear (the Son of Man's) voice and come out— those who have done good will rise to live, and those who have done evil will rise to be condemned."

- The voice of the archangel seems to be a reference to the hordes of angels surrounding the Son of Man that Jesus spoke about.

- The great trumpet blast is spoken of most in the Hebrew Scriptures. At the festivals looking forward to the victory of the New Creation, the trumpet blasts would be sounded.[5] On that final day, as Jesus the Son of Man finally descends to His eternal home, *God Himself* will sound a mighty trumpet to announce the defeat of all evil.

Paul tells the Thessalonians all this to reassure them that they cannot possibly miss all this when it happens. Sometimes cults have taught that Jesus *secretly* returned and then went away again. We must reject all this heresy, because when Jesus returns we will *hear* it very clearly.

The dead Christians returning with Jesus will receive their bodies first (verse 16b), but the Christians still alive on the earth will not be far behind. They too will join the Son of Man coming with the clouds of heaven (Daniel 7:13). So, whether we are dead or alive at the time of Jesus' return, none of us will miss out on the resurrection of our bodies or our everlasting future on the renewed earth. As Paul says, after we have all met together, joining in Jesus return, so "we will be with the Lord forever."

These *are* very encouraging words (verse 18). We need have no fears about death. We will not miss out on anything regardless of when we die.

The LORD Jesus will gather together all His followers of every age even as He is coming from heaven to earth.

He wants every one of us to be fully included in every single moment of that glorious resurrection future.

---

[5] See Leviticus 25:9; Psalm 81:3. But also read Exodus 19:10-20 for a clear statement that the trumpet sound heralds the descent of the LORD to the earth. Note the trumpet blasts in the defeat of Jericho in Joshua chapter 6 – the victory of the LORD over His enemies.

b.   Times and Dates (1 Thessalonians 5:1-3)

There are always those who think that they have discovered what even Jesus Himself does not know – the date of His return. When the disciples questioned Jesus about this He told them very plainly (Mark 13:32-33) "no-one knows about that day or hour, not even the angels in heaven, nor the Son, but only the Father. Be on guard! Be alert! You do not know when that time will come." Again in Acts 1:7, just before He ascended to heaven, He told them. "it is not for you to know the times or dates the Father has set by his own authority."

The Son will return the very moment that the Father tells Him to do so. If the Son is content to leave the matter entirely in the hands of the Father, we must certainly do the same.

Paul, then, is warning us not to get caught up in the feverish fads of prediction that Christians sometimes get caught in. In fact, verse 3, Jesus' return will come at a time when people least expect, at a time when people feel safe and peaceful. The trauma of His return is as inevitable as labour pains in a pregnancy. Paul's image captures the way in which the pregnant woman can so quickly go from peace to pain as soon as the labour pains begin. The parallel goes further: labour pains also are quickly followed by the birth of a new life. The pains of the end of the age will certainly be followed by the wonderful life of the renewed creation.

c.   Night and Day (1 Thessalonians 5:4-11)

Having warned us how unexpected Jesus' return will be, he wants to reassure the Thessalonians that the Christians do not need to fear that day in any way. Firstly, the return of Jesus is not our destruction, but our liberation. Secondly, as sons of the light and day, we are *always* ready for Jesus return. For us He is not like an unexpected thief breaking into our home, but the home-owner returning to reward His faithful servants and get rid of the thieves in His house! (Compare Mark 13:34-37).

We are not sleeping in the night, unaware of the approaching danger (verse 5-6). Rather, we are awake and alert, fully aware of what is happening, fully *ready* for the inevitable return of the Lord.

The Bible, right from Genesis chapter 1, analyses the world according to day and night. The night time is the time of chaos and disorder. Sinful activity and unbelief belongs to the night. For example, in John 3 unbelieving Nicodemus comes to Jesus *at night*, but in John 4 the woman believes in Jesus *at noon*. So, here, Paul divides the world into day and night – the Christians live in the day with self-control, whereas the non-Christian lives in the night without self-control.

We are ready and equipped for the future (verse 8), "wearing" the gospel at all times. We *trust* Jesus, *love* each other and *hope* for Jesus return. The person who lives with such faith, love and hope has nothing to fear from Jesus' return. The Christian will not face Jesus' wrath (verse 9), but rather will receive a wonderful liberation on that final day. Our days of sin and persecution will be gone forever, and we will enjoy the creation with Jesus, as the human race was originally intended to do.

The purpose of Jesus' death was that all those who trust in Him, whether they are still alive or long dead, may live together with Him forever (verse 10). If we trust in His death, then we should be certain of that future… and we should keep encouraging each other with this truth.

The return of Jesus and our future together with Him should be a frequent theme in our conversations. Sometimes Christians are ignorant of this future and treat it all as a vague and unknowable subject. This is a very wrong attitude. The Scriptures describe our future so carefully and in so much detail precisely so that we can think and talk a great deal about it. This is the subject that will really affect the way we live our lives right now. For the joy set before us we endure any and every cost of the present.

d. Through and Through (1 Thessalonians 5:12-28)

Verse 23 – "May God himself, the God of peace, sanctify you through and through. May your whole spirit, soul and body be kept blameless at the coming of our Lord Jesus Christ." *That* is our theme verse in this section. We have been *spiritually* born again, our *souls* (Greek 'psyche', i.e. *mind*) are being renewed as we follow Jesus, and our *bodies* await redemption at the return of Jesus. Past, present and future – our spiritual new birth in the past; the present ongoing change in our thinking; our future resurrection. Our goal is resurrection morning when all these "parts" of us are completely conformed to Jesus. Paul's long description of how we should live as we await our glorious future can all be captured in verse 23.

He begins with the organisation of the local Christian family. The hard-working Bible teachers ensure the faithful living of the church family. These leaders need plenty of love and respect. So many local churches are crippled as the leaders are constantly undermined. Paul begins at this point because it is through this Biblical leadership that all the other aspects of our living are guarded and developed. The grumbler will not only be fruitless in their own life, but they will inflict their barrenness on the rest of the church family.

Instead of arguing and grumbling, we should (verse 13b) "live in peace with each other." That does *not* mean that we should just ignore each other. Rather we should work hard to help and encourage each other, with warnings to the lazy, encouragements for the timid, all kinds of practical help for the weak or ill, and, of course, lots and lots of patience for *everyone*.

How do we prevent destructive arguments and feuds? The answer is simple, even if it is difficult to put into practice. Verse 15, we must not retaliate when we are wronged. Instead, when someone does wrong to us we should pay them back with kindness. This is a real test of Christian maturity and spiritual power. If we want to see the miraculous, almighty power of the Spirit in our local church, then we should pray hard for this to happen. Nothing so demonstrates the reality of the gospel than paying back kindness for evil.

Joy is compulsory in the Christian life. Whether we like it or not we *must* be joyful! If we think about our future hope and the way we have been rescued from Hell, then how can we not be joyful, even in the most difficult circumstances? It is very likely we have all seen examples of this joy in the Spirit from people who have many, many reasons to be very sad indeed. It is important to remember that they do not have a special gift of joy. Rather, they are laying hold of and appreciating the joy that we all have in the Spirit.

Paul develops this theme so that we can see *how* to be joyful at all times. In all circumstances we are to be praying our thanks to God. Our blessings in Jesus always infinitely outweigh the pain and troubles of this passing age. The joyful heart is the grateful heart. The ungrateful Christian will be a joyless Christian. It is this ingratitude that quenches the Spirit (verse 19).

"do not treat prophecies with contempt." (verse 20). Matthew Henry, the great 18th century Bible scholar explains this well: "By prophesyings here we are to understand the preaching of the word, the interpreting and applying of the scriptures; and this we must not despise, but should prize and value, because it is the ordinance of God, appointed of him for our furtherance and increase in knowledge and grace, in holiness and comfort."

If we are properly instructed in the Scriptures, so we can test everything (verse 21). We can see what is good and worth holding onto, but we can also avoid every kind of evil (verse 22). We dare not make these judgements with our own personal theories, but only with the mind of Jesus shown to us in the Bible.

Paul concludes the letter with this wonderful assurance that faithful Jesus (verse 24) will certainly deliver us all safely and thoroughly sanctified to our eternal home. Paul has prayed so much for these

Thessalonians, and now he briefly asks that they will pray for Paul, Silas and Timothy (verse 25).

Verse 26 causes concern for those who do not like to show their affection. Paul has asked them to love each other, repetitively. If we are a loving *family* then greeting one another with a kiss is a completely natural thing to do. Perhaps some of us are not yet ready for this advanced church life, but Paul is encouraging us to keep going until we get there! The friendship of Jesus is with us (verse 28) and that surely inspires us to love one another at least as much as flesh and blood families love each other.

Study 4   Bible Questions

1 Thessalonians 5:12-18

1. Paul has been writing about the second coming of Jesus since 4:13. What is the link between that and verses 12-13?

2. In what ways can you support the leaders of your church? How should we deal with being corrected?

3. So often the Bible tells us to love each other and not quarrel. Why is this so important? What's the difference between actively loving each other on the one hand, and on the other simply tolerating each other without arguments? (See John 17:23; 1 John 4:19-21)

4. Verse 14 – if it was your job to warn the idle believer, what would you say? Think about the context of these verses – 5:4-11.

5. It is very hard not to retaliate when someone does us wrong. How does the Bible teach us that we can live out verse 15? Look at Paul's words in Romans 12:17-21.

6. To understand the importance of always living out verses 16-18, let us look at the story of Job. Satan believed that Job was only trusting the Lord out of self-interest. How do we see that in Job 1:8-11?

7. Look at Job's faithful response to the Lord even after he has lost all his possessions and some of his family have been killed, Job 1:20-22; 2:10. How does Job's godly response defeat Satan's attack? And how does it teach us the power of verses 16-18 in our passage of 1 Thessalonians 5?

8. How will what you have learned today change your life from now on?

Study 4   Further Questions

1. How should we grieve when fellow Christians die? How is it different?

2. In recent years it has become quite popular to think of Christians *secretly* disappearing to meet Jesus in the sky a few years before the real return of Jesus. What would the apostle Paul think about this?

3. In 1 Thessalonians 4:23 Paul describes us as made up of 3 things: body, soul and spirit. Some have argued that soul and spirit are the same thing so that we are really made of just two parts. Which view seems best and does it matter?

Study 4   Daily Readings

Day 1	1 Thessalonians 4:13-5:28
Day 2	Matthew 24:1-35
Day 3	Matthew 24:36-51
Day 4	Isaiah chapter 11
Day 5	Matthew chapter 25
Day 6	Ephesians 4:17-32
Day 7	Job chapter 1

The daily Bible readings are an opportunity to not only read through all of the material in the book under study, but also to read parts of the Bible that relate to the themes and issues that we have been considering. We try to make sure that we receive light from the whole Bible as we think through the key issues each week.

The antichrist revealed

2 Thessalonians 1:1-2:12

> **Key Truth:** Glory will come after we have been faithful in suffering for our Lord. Jesus will return and all the deceiving work of Satan will be destroyed.

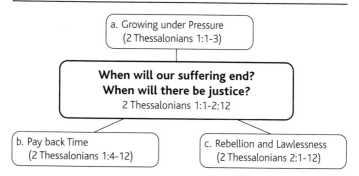

a. Growing under Pressure
(2 Thessalonians 1:1-3)

When will our suffering end?
When will there be justice?
2 Thessalonians 1:1-2:12

b. Pay back Time
(2 Thessalonians 1:4-12)

c. Rebellion and Lawlessness
(2 Thessalonians 2:1-12)

a.   Growing under Pressure (2 Thessalonians 1:1-3)

Paul, Silas & Timothy begin the second letter with great encouragement for the Thessalonians. They were clearly very encouraged about the progress that this pioneer church was making, but they also knew that those new Christians were very isolated against severe opposition. So, like the first letter, the first two verses strongly emphasise that the Thessalonian church is still surrounded by God the Father and the LORD Jesus Christ.

They had prayed that the Thessalonians would love more and more [6]... and already that prayer had been answered (verse 3). Under the kind of persecution and pressure that they were experiencing it is a true mark of spiritual life that they were able to trust Jesus more strongly and love each other more deeply.

If we want to assess a person's spiritual maturity we don't need to give them a doctrine test or ask about their special experiences.

---

[6] 1 Thessalonians 3:12

Rather we need to see the impact of Jesus on their day-to-day lives and the way they love the Christian family. It is never a good sign when a Christian prefers non-Christian company.

b. Pay back Time (2 Thessalonians 1:4-12)

God has made a judgement about the way His people should be tested and glorified (verse 5). The judgement of the Father is that glory comes *after* faithfulness in suffering. This pattern was established in the life, death, resurrection and ascension of Jesus. Jesus knew that His vindication and glory would come only through the way of the Cross. The Father has set up the world and history in such a way that we share in the future glory of His Messiah after we have faithfully shared in His sufferings.

In his letter to the Romans, Paul describes this as the mark of being true children of the Living God:

> **Romans 8:17-18** "Now if we are children, then we are heirs — heirs of God and co-heirs with Christ, if indeed *we share in his sufferings in order that we may also share in his glory.* I consider that our present sufferings are not worth comparing with the glory that will be revealed in us."

The apostle Peter says that the OT prophets were looking forward to the Messiah demonstrating *this* key feature of spiritual life. In 1 Peter 1:11 he describes the way the prophets were "trying to find out the time and circumstances to which the Spirit of Christ in them was pointing when he predicted *the sufferings of Christ and the glories that would follow."*

Faithfulness to the Messiah in suffering followed by future glory is at the very heart of discipleship throughout the whole Bible.

The reality of our trust in the Messiah is shown when we forsake our present lives, money, security, popularity and status for the great glory and affirmation that we will receive when Jesus returns. People may *claim* to be trusting in Jesus, but we see the truth behind those words when they really *live* in the light of His glorious return.

So, here Paul is pointing out that the growth in trust and love shown in the Thessalonians proves that the Father's way of dealing with His people is right. Even under severe pressure the reality of the Thessalonians' new life shines out. Defying all human explanation, the Thessalonian church was a kind of "boasting" point for the gospel (verse 4).

Nothing shows the truth of God's gospel so much as this faithful growth under pressure.

However, whereas the Church *now* endures the persecution and ridicule of unbelievers, this situation has a very definite end. When Jesus returns all appearances are overturned. The despised Christians will be glorified with Jesus and those who have harmed the Christians will find themselves receiving pay-back – "God is just: He will pay back trouble to those who trouble you" (verse 6).

The Christians will receive wonderful relief and eternal comfort when Jesus returns, but those who do not trust Him will face serious trouble. He left earth in humility and quietness. He will return in blazing fire with a powerful angelic army. There will be no escape or resistance. Jesus is the judge of the world and He will bring punishment to humanity. What is the crime that requires such terrible punishment?

"He will punish those who do not know God and do not obey the gospel of our Lord Jesus" (2 Thessalonians 1:8).

Paul makes it clear that anyone who does not obey Jesus' gospel does not know God. Much of the Western Christian world is not used to being surrounded by powerful and sophisticated religions. Most Christians in the world have experienced this for hundreds of years. However, one of the cultural pressures in the West is to assume that all religions are just different ways of knowing God. Jesus is expected to take His place alongside other options.[7]

---

[7] Some say that although Jesus is the only way, He will save those who sincerely follow human religions.

Paul brings us back to reality. Jesus is the LORD and Judge over the whole world. The Father has set a day when He will send Jesus to bring terrible punishment on the whole human race. Humanity's rejection of God will end with an eternal separation in Hell (verse 9).

There is only one possible escape from the coming judgement and punishment. The gospel of Jesus is the amazingly good news that our Judge has made it possible, through His own death, to escape from the Day of God's Anger and Justice. This is why so many Christians have been prepared to lay down their lives to tell unreached people the good news.

If this does not encourage us to make the way of escape known to everybody we can, then our hearts are truly dead.

When Jesus returns those who have trusted Him will marvel at Him (verse 10) and we will actually share His divine glory. Yes, anyone who trusts the gospel will, like the Thessalonians, be gathered into the glory of Jesus when He returns on the Day of Judgement. For us there will be no fear on that day: it will be a day of great joy and affirmation.

Matthew Henry, the 18th century Bible scholar, comments on this chapter by emphasising how certain we must be about Jesus' return:

> It is most certain that the Lord Jesus Christ will come to judge the world, that he will come in all the pomp and power of the upper world in the last day, to execute judgment upon all. Whatever uncertainty we have, or whatever mistakes may arise about the time of his coming, his coming itself is certain. This has been the faith and hope of all Christians in all ages of the church; nay, it was the faith and hope of the Old-Testament saints, ever since Enoch the seventh from Adam, who said, Behold, the Lord cometh, etc., Jude 14.

It is important to notice the connection between verse 5 and verse 10. In verse 5 Paul speaks of being found "worthy of the kingdom of God". In verse 10 we find that those who have believed in Jesus are the ones who will be found worthy when He returns. In other words, *we* cannot make *ourselves* worthy. It is our Saviour *Jesus* who makes us worthy through His life, death and resurrection.

So, with this clear description of the *future* of the Thessalonians, Paul turns to their *current* lives. His prayer is that they will keep trusting Jesus and be enabled to live this faith out (verse 11). If they do this then Jesus will already be glorified through them right now among all their pressure and persecution, but they will also share His glory at His return through the grace of the Father and Jesus.

c.   Rebellion and Lawlessness (2 Thessalonians 2:1-12)

Paul began with the key truths about the future that would most encourage the Thessalonians. The injustice and cruelty that they were receiving now would all be put right when Jesus returned.

Now, Paul turns to some more detailed concerns that they had about the return of Jesus. It seems that they had heard, possibly through a letter that claimed to be from Paul himself (verse 2), that Jesus had already returned. Perhaps they imagined that Jesus had returned to Jerusalem and had begun to establish His kingdom on earth in opposition to the kingdoms of this world. If this were so the Thessalonians would want to leave and join Him, or at least give up all their normal activities. Why bother doing any work if Jesus was already unleashing His irresistible force against the passing human systems? Surely the only thing worth doing was waiting around for His kingdom of immortality and glory to arrive at Thessalonica.

Paul had told the Thessalonians that everyone in the world will know the moment Jesus returns (1 Thess 4:16). It will not be a secret or merely local event. Furthermore, certain things have to happen in the history of the church before Jesus will return.

In 2 Thessalonians 2:5 Paul says that he told them all about this while he was with them for that month. It seems most likely that he simply told them what Jesus had said about this. If we read Matthew 24 we see Jesus warning His disciples about the future:

> **Matthew 24:24-31** "For *false Christs* and false prophets will appear and perform great signs and miracles to deceive even the elect – if that were possible. See, I have told you ahead of time... For as lightning that comes from the east is visible even in the west, so will be the coming of the Son of Man... Immediately after *the distress* of those days `the sun will be darkened, and the moon will not give its light; the stars will fall from the sky, and the heavenly bodies will be shaken.' At that time the sign of the Son of Man will appear in the sky, and all the nations of the earth will mourn. They will see the Son of Man coming on the clouds of the sky, with power and great glory. And he will send his angels with a loud trumpet call, and they will gather his elect from the four winds, from one end of the heavens to the other."

All that Paul has taught in these letters can be found in that speech of Jesus. Notice that Jesus indicates that there will be a terrible time ("the distress") just before He returns.

Paul is not dreaming up new information in his Thessalonian letters, but explaining the original teaching of Jesus.

In verses 3-4 Paul says that there will be a rebellion in which a "man of lawlessness" will try to take the place of God in "the temple of God". When Paul speaks of "the temple of God" (verse 4) it seems that he is speaking about the Church. In Ephesians 2:19-21 he speaks of the church as a temple. We see the same thing in 2 Corinthians 6:16 – "What agreement is there between the temple of God and idols? For we are the temple of the living God. As God has said: 'I will live with them and walk among them, and I will be their God, and they will be my people.'"

So, it seems that the "man of lawlessness" will demand allegiance within the Church, but will be in opposition to the Living God. He is the ultimate false teacher.

When we think about lawlessness we might think about violence on the streets, corporate greed, drug culture, sexual immorality or political deception. All these things do indicate a chaotic rebellion against the Living God, but Jesus shows us the real heart of lawlessness in Matthew 23:28. Speaking to the very respectable Bible students of his day He said, "on the outside you appear to people as righteous but on the inside you are full of hypocrisy and wickedness *(lawlessness)."*

Lawlessness in *our* eyes is often simply what disrupts *our own* comfort and stability. Ultimate lawlessness in the eyes of the Father, Son and Holy Spirit is much deeper and more pervasive. According to Jesus, lawlessness can fill the hearts of those who are careful to obey *human* laws.

When we see a respectable church leader who denies the truth in Jesus, we must recognise that they are part of this lawless, rebellion. History has been filled with these "false Christs", leaders who try to take the place of Jesus, teaching truths that undermine the gospel. Until Jesus' return, there will be these men of lawlessness, but it seems that they are all perhaps just warnings, precursors of one final person who will be the final and ultimate anti-Christ, the most dangerous of all – the man of lawlessness.

The apostle John also speaks of this pattern of history. *1 John 2:18* "Dear children, this is the last hour; and as you have heard that *the antichrist* is coming, even now many antichrists have come. This is how we know it is the last hour."

The antichrist, the man of lawlessness… who will it be? Is he already on the world stage? Or has this already happened? There have been more than enough examples in the history of the Church where a large proportion of the Church has rebelliously followed false teaching. If the apostle Paul saw the way the Western church murdered thousands of people in the name of Christ in the crusades, or the vain superstition of many churches in history, or the devilish materialism of modern churches, would he believe that The Rebellion had already happened?

One thing is clear, the faithful followers of Jesus need to be on their guard not only from persecution from outside the church but also from false teaching and compromise within the church. When we see church leaders full of their own importance or so-called Christians questioning the Bible's teaching or lining their pockets with money or compromising with pagan culture... then we know that the lawless rebellion of 2 Thessalonians is threatening us. Whether it is the sophisticated intellectual or the mindless hedonist, it is always the same spirit of antichrist.

Paul warned the Thessalonians about this (verse 5), but indicated that the time of this rebellion was being held back (verse 6-7). The "secret power of lawlessness" was already at work (verse 7) and Paul had seen enough false teaching and unbelieving life-styles in the Church to know this. However, the final rebellion was being held back. *Who* or *what* is holding it back?

Well, in verses 9-10 we see that *Satan* is behind the lawlessness. Satan will use all his power, even performing miracles, in order to deceive humanity. Satan is called the Destroyer (Rev. 9:11) because he wants humanity to perish with him on the Day of Judgement. If he can prevent people from believing in Jesus, then they will share his fate in the lake of fire.

So, *who* is holding Satan back? *Who* is preventing his *deceptions* from controlling the whole human race? In verse 13 we see that *God the Spirit* is at work to make us holy and to make us believe the *truth*. It would make sense to see the Spirit limiting the work of Satan, until the very end when Satan will be unmasked and then destroyed.

The Thessalonians were loved, saved, chosen and sanctified (verse 13) through the gospel (verse 14). This underlines the precious value of the gospel. In a world where the deceptions of Satan lead a willing humanity into Hell, there is only one way of escape and freedom – the gospel of Jesus applied by the almighty Holy Spirit.

The wickedness of humanity is shown in that we prefer to believe the deceptions of the devil and refuse "to love the truth". The Father judges this evil choice by giving humanity over to our evil choices and allowing the devil to continue his deception (verses 11-12). The Bible repetitively teaches us that when we choose evil the Living God lets us slip deeper into the blindness and delusion of evil.[8] We end up *delighting* in wickedness, which reveals how right God is to be so very angry at what we have become.

The key truth for us to know is in verse 8. We might be feeling a little overwhelmed or nervous about the power of Satan and the lawless human rebellion. However, we need to know that all this opposition to Jesus is utterly futile and weak in the end. When He returns He will completely destroy all His enemies with simply His bright appearance and the breath of His mouth. He will only have to *blow* on them to defeat them!

---

[8] See Romans 1:24-28

Study 5   Bible Questions

2 Thessalonians 1:3-10

1. From verse 3, what is Paul's goal for his fellow believers? Do we share this and praise the LORD when we see it happen?

2. What do you think Paul would have said when he 'boasted' (verse 4) about the Thessalonian church? How might this compare to our own assessment of churches?

3. What lessons does Paul draw from verse 4 for (a) the Thessalonians, (b) other Christians, (c) unbelievers? (See verses 5-6)

4. How can we as Christians endure suffering? Why not walk away, or blame God?

5. Look at the description of Jesus in verses 7-9. Many people refuse to think of Jesus as the powerful frightening King of the world. Why is it important to our faith, prayer life and evangelism that we do recognise Jesus in this way? (For a fuller description, see Revelation 1:12-18 and Revelation 19:11-16)

6. How would you explain the link in verse 8, between 'knowing God' and the 'gospel of Jesus'. Is it possible to know God as an unbeliever? (Matthew 11:25-27)

7. Look at what will happen to Christians when Jesus returns, verse 10. How should this sure hope encourage us to live?

Study 5   Further Questions

1. Paul encourages us with the knowledge that those who trouble us now will get serious trouble when Jesus returns. Does this create a tension with Jesus' teaching about turning the other cheek from Matthew 5:39? Are these two truths actually joined together?

2. Think about the different views of "the man of lawlessness". Set out the arguments for and against these different theories. Could Paul be referring to a single world leader? Could it be a global church leader? Could it be a famous historical person like Emperor Nero, Joseph Stalin, Adolf Hitler etc?

3. Is it helpful to tell the non-Christian world all about the return of Jesus? If we talk about the eternal punishment they will face, would we simply be accused of "scaring people into the kingdom"? Is that a wrong thing to do?

Study 5   Daily Readings

Day 1	2 Thessalonians 1-2:12
Day 2	Romans 8:17-39
Day 3	Psalm 33
Day 4	Revelation 1:4-20
Day 5	Daniel chapter 10
Day 6	1 John chapter 2
Day 7	Revelation chapter 19

The daily Bible readings are an opportunity to not only read through all of the material in the book under study, but also to read parts of the Bible that relate to the themes and issues that we have been considering. We try to make sure that we receive light from the whole Bible as we think through the key issues each week.

Study 6   How are you going to wait?

The Great Falling Away

2 Thessalonians 2:13-3:17

Key Truth: As the Church waits for Jesus to return, we work hard to see the gospel message shared with others, turning away from disobedient and idle lifestyles.

a. Sharing in the glory of Jesus
(2 Thessalonians 2:13-17)

d. Family Discipline
(2 Thessalonians 3:14-18)

How are you going to wait?
2 Thessalonians 2:13-3:17

b. Protected and Obedient
(2 Thessalonians 3:1-5)

c. Busy and Productive Lives
(2 Thessalonians 3:6-12)

a. Sharing in the glory of Jesus (2 Thessalonians 2:13-17)

Through the gospel we can become a loved family member of the Living God instead of a doomed enemy. Paul thanks the Father for this wonderful alternative that the Church has in Jesus by the power of the Spirit (verse 13). We can share in Jesus' glory (verse 14) rather than perish with the devil and his lies. We should always be full of wonder and gratitude for the gospel.

Without the life, death and resurrection of Jesus we would all face the righteous judgement of eternal punishment.

Without the gospel the human race is an utterly hopeless, lawless, pointless existence.

With the gospel we can find not only mercy but a share in Jesus' glory! We don't deserve such a wonderful future, but out of sheer over-flowing love it is a free gift everybody can receive simply by trusting Jesus.

The proper response to this is our passionate commitment to the apostles' teaching. It was the mark of the believers after the Day of Pentecost in Acts 2:42. So, verse 15, we will stand firm against outward persecution and inner rebellious temptations only as we hold firm to the apostolic teaching. Of course, this means that we must regularly and carefully and obediently read the Bible.

If we do not *daily* shape our minds and lives by this divine truth, then we will be shaped instead by the deceptions of the devil all around us. Alone, left to our own thinking, we will fall into Satan's traps. As Paul prays in verses 16-17, we need the LORD Jesus and God the Father to encourage us. If our words and actions are going to be consistently *good* (verse 17), then we need the encouragement of our "good hope" (which Paul has told us so much about) and divine strength.

b. Protected and Obedient (2 Thessalonians 3:1-5)

Paul is intensely aware of this deep dependence on the power and truth of the Living God. He knew that there was no hope in merely human strength and wisdom. This is why he asks for prayer from these Thessalonians. Prayer is the sign that we understand ourselves and the world.

If we don't pray it means that we think we are strong enough and wise enough to manage on our own. The basic feature of prayer is recognising that we cannot do anything of any value unless the Living God works through us.

So, Paul's first prayer request is for the work of evangelism. If the gospel is the only hope for the human race, then it is vital that it "spread rapidly and be honoured". Paul was desperate to get the gospel out to the very places that no one had been to before.[9]

---

[9] Romans 15:19-20 "So from Jerusalem all the way round to Illyricum, I have fully proclaimed the gospel of Christ. It has always been my ambition to preach the gospel where Christ was not known...

Paul's second prayer request was for protection from the enemies of the gospel. Notice that he assumes that anyone who does not have faith in Jesus is "wicked and evil". It seems a harsh verdict to a modern ear, but we are not used to thinking of the world in the way that the Living God does. We must remember how Paul described the human race earlier in this letter. Without Jesus we all delight in wickedness, refuse to follow the gospel and believe the deceptions of Satan. We need divine protection once we have committed our lives to telling our neighbours and colleagues about Jesus. Satan will stir up trouble against us. We need to constantly pray for each other to be delivered from Satan's schemes.

We can pray with great confidence in this matter, because (verse 3) the LORD is faithful to us and *wants* to give us strength and protection from Satan. As we depend on Jesus so He will never let us down.

We are *waiting* for Jesus to return... but we are *not wasting* our time.

We use our time to bring as many people into the safety of the gospel as we possibly can before it is too late. Satan opposes us, but as we trust Jesus and do His will, shown to us in the Scriptures, so we will persevere to the end. Paul had confidence that the Thessalonians would keep going (verse 4). However, he prays in verse 5 that Jesus would turn their *hearts* to love God the Father and persevere in Him. It is very important that we love the Father and do not love the passing distractions of this passing age.

Whatever we love will determine the course of our lives. If we love the Father and long for that final day when Jesus will enable Him to come and live with us here, then we will be able to avoid all the deceptions of Satan who *wants* us to waste our lives trying to build our own heaven on earth right now.

c.   Busy and Productive Lives (2 Thessalonians 3:6-12)

We learned in 2 Thess. 2:2 that the Thessalonians had received a false report that Jesus had already returned. The Thessalonians seemed to like the idea of living a life of leisure, so presumably this had made some of them give up on normal day-to-day work. Why bother with our careers if it is all about to be overthrown by Jesus?

In this next section Paul shows us the balanced life. On the one hand we must lay down our lives in eager expectation of Jesus' return, but on the other hand we must keep engaged with the normal run of daily life in this passing age. We are to be productive and valued members of the societies we live in, even though we are driven by a very different hope.

Paul begins by equating laziness with disobeying the apostles' teaching. In fact, he says that we must cut off any Christian who lives a lazy life. Their lifestyle undermines and discredits the gospel, so we must make it clear to the watching world that they do *not* represent the gospel of God. Paul and his friends had shown them how to live in the month they had been there (verse 7). They made sure that they were paying their way among the Thessalonians. They worked really hard so that they were not taking away other people's hard-earned cash.

As a minister of the gospel, Paul's job deserved to receive a proper salary (verse 9)[10], but he could see that the temptation among the Thessalonians was to give up on labour and simply live off other people's resources. When Paul and Silas had been with them, they had given them a simple rule for productive living: anybody who doesn't want to work, doesn't get to eat. These words have been taken out of context many times and used in all kinds of political slogans. Nevertheless they give us an important truth. We must see to it that our Christian family is busy and productive.

Whether we have big salaries, tight budgets or even work in unpaid labour, our lives must be characterised as busy and productive. If we are not doing this, then Paul warns us, we are likely to be

---

[10] See also 1 Timothy 5:17-18.

"busybodies". We may have heard the popular saying: the devil makes work for idle hands. This teaching of Paul could be the origin of that saying.

If we are not *contributing* to the Christian family, then we are *undermining* it.

Paul is not alone in this teaching. The book of Proverbs in the Bible has much to say about the deadly dangers of laziness. In the modern world, many people live simply for leisure. They dream of earning or winning enough money to do nothing, to simply spend all day pleasing themselves. The Word of God warns us very directly and sternly against all such aspirations.

d.   Family Discipline (2 Thessalonians 3:14-18)

The letter concludes with some of the clearest teaching in the whole Bible on how we are to deal with one another when a fellow Christian refuses to repent of their sin.

Paul begins by encouraging us to never tire of doing what is right. We must live busy and productive lives, working to spread the gospel and caring for each other. Satan will always whisper into our ear that we don't need to bother with all this. He will always tempt us with dreams of a comfortable life of pleasure and popularity. We mustn't forget that he is deceiving us into the barren, pointless, hopeless doom that is all his future holds.

However, what do we do when a fellow Christian does fall into lawless disobedience? The problem is not a Christian *sinning*, but *refusing to repent* of their sin. As long as our brother or sister turns away from their sin, then we encourage them with the warmest fellowship.[11] On the other hand, if they actually reject the Word of God (in this case Paul's letter), then we are to take the matter very

---

[11] Of course, someone who pretends to turn from their sin but endlessly repeats it is not repenting at all. Repentance means taking our sin very seriously. We must take every possible measure in order to turn away from our sin. In Christ there is freedom from sin... but never licence to sin.

seriously. We are not to have any fellowship at all with such a person, not because we don't care about them, but so that we can help them to feel ashamed of their wickedness. We want to embrace this Christian back into the Church family, but their rejection of the Bible's teaching means that they have placed themselves outside. By making them deeply aware of the consequences of their sin, we may be able to remind them of the truth.[12]

We are not to think of this sinful Christian as an enemy (verse 15), but keep pleading with him to turn from his error. He is still our Christian brother even though he has turned away from the Church family.

It takes a lot of love and commitment to each other to put this into practice. The constant temptation is to simply gossip about one another or ignore one another. To actually put verse 14 into practice means that we have to really care about the faithful endurance of every family member. If we are used to Church being nothing more than a once-a-week couple of hours in an old building, then the Bible's vision of Church life will need a revolution in our living.

In verse 17 Paul lets them know that they can trust this letter as a genuine Pauline letter, because he wrote it (or at least signed it) *personally*.

In these two letters we have seen the Thessalonian church under severe persecution from enemies of the gospel. Satan is at work to undermine them and deceive them into lawless rebellion. They are also threatened from within by laziness and false teaching. It might seem to be a situation of turmoil and anguish, but that is not how we end the letter.

---

[12] Consider the problem of domestic abuse. It is not right for a wife to endlessly endure abuse. That doesn't help herself, her children or her husband. He has to live with the true consequences of his actions as the wife and children find safety with family, friends or social services. This may be what brings him to an understanding of what he has done and seeks the proper oversight and counselling that he needs. In this way it may be possible to restore the family.

In verse 16 Paul writes one of the most wonderful blessings in the Bible – "May the Lord of peace Himself give you peace at *all times* and in *every way*. The Lord be with all of you."

Peace at all times in every way. That is what it is like to live in fellowship with Jesus, the LORD of peace. To us, through the gospel, He is not the Judge full of fiery anger, but our Loving Lord whose presence gives us indescribable peace in every situation.

Study 6   Bible Questions

2 Thessalonians 3:6-15

1. According to these verses, why is Paul so against idleness?

2. How can being idle have a negative effect on our evangelism, and our own relationship with Jesus?

3. Look at verses 8-9. What did Paul and his team sacrifice and why? In what ways can we follow their example to benefit our church family?

4. It is especially bad when a Christian is a busybody, verse 11. Our message to unbelievers is not 'lead a more moral life'. Why not? What wrong idea would this give about the gospel message?

5. Verses 14-15 seem quite harsh. How would putting this into practice actually be a very loving thing to do? How much commitment would it take in your local church?

6. What have you learnt about the Thessalonian Christians from our studies in 1&2 Thessalonians? What will impact your life the most?

Study 6   Further Questions

1. If we have enough money to "pay our own way", then do we still need to live busy and productive lives? What should we spend our time and money doing?

2. If a member of the fellowship has no paid work, how can they continue to be busy and productive? What can they do that will help the world to see that glory of the gospel in the life of the Church?

3. If a member of our Church disobeys the Bible and refuses to repent, what would we do if they just decided to go to another church in the area who didn't know about their sin? What implications does this have for unity among all the Bible-teaching churches?

Study 6	Daily Readings
Day 1	2 Thessalonians 2:13-3:17
Day 2	Acts 2:36-47
Day 3	Proverbs 6:1-19
Day 4	1 Timothy 5:17-6:10
Day 5	Proverbs chapter 19
Day 6	Romans chapter 6
Day 7	Philippians 4:4-13

The daily Bible readings are an opportunity to not only read through all of the material in the book under study, but also to read parts of the Bible that relate to the themes and issues that we have been considering. We try to make sure that we receive light from the whole Bible as we think through the key issues each week.

4 Suggested Answers to the Bible Study Questions

Study 1   Bible Answers

1 Thessalonians 1:2-10

1. Faith, love and hope in the Lord Jesus Christ.

2. We trust in the Father's care for us, knowing that He will not let us down as we obey Him. We love one another and know that we are loved by the Living God. We have the certain hope that no matter what we face in this passing age, we have a glorious future in Jesus.

3. Our prayers should begin with thanks, remembering all the blessings that God has given to our fellow Christians. We should also pray for the fruit of the Spirit – faith, love and hope – to flourish in them. We should avoid prayers that are simple lists of immediate needs.

4. The Word of God had a genuine effect in their lives. They began to genuinely imitate the lifestyle of the apostles, which is the way of Jesus. They were a model of Jesus to the surrounding area. We can see the reality of people by the fruit they produce.

5. They had accepted the reasoning of Scripture as they believed in Jesus, when they went to the synagogue to hear Paul. Jason welcomed the apostolic party into his house. They endured opposition for Jesus.

6. It seems as if the Thessalonian church wanted to proclaim the good news in Macedonia and Achaia. Perhaps they sent people like Jason to explain the message in those other cities. Their lifestyle was also an essential part of their evangelism. They made it clear that they had turned from idols to the Living God. Many other people began to talk about the 'gospel revolution' at Thessalonica.

7. What teaching of Jesus is most against the assumptions of our culture or neighbourhood? Giving our possessions to those who need it? Bible study? Caring for neighbours? Visiting the sick? Praying for people? Helping asylum seekers? Street evangelism? The way we spend our money and use our time reveals everything about us: what we value; what we dream of; who we care about.

Study 2   Bible Answers

1 Thessalonians 2:1-12

1. They see life very differently. Suffering and opposition are no longer seen as failure. They are able and willing to bear hardship for Jesus, because of 'the help of our God'.

2. Jesus Himself told us that if the world hated Him (and He is the nicest Person who has ever lived!), then the world will certainly also hate us. Following Jesus means following His way of the Cross. It seems to be that the truth and power of the gospel is only really shown as our lives are broken open as we share with Jesus in that way of obedience and joy.

3. We all have mixed motives... even in our best service. However, we must never be side-tracked by the desire for popularity or money or power. We must guard our hearts to ensure that God's approval means far more to us than anything else.

4. We are ambassadors of the Living God – in whom is not even the tiniest trace of darkness. We cannot pretend that our own actions do not 'colour' the pure gospel message. If we are corrupt or deceitful in our presentation then the world could conclude that our God is corrupt or deceitful! We should always tell the simple truth and leave it to the Living God to convince the world.

5. Sharing the gospel is far more than sharing 'information'. As ambassadors of Jesus, our lives are the 'posters' that declare Jesus to those around us. More important than winning all the arguments is showing the gentle, humble and loving way of Jesus. Working hard for the sake of others wins respect. If we neglect our family out of 'zeal for Jesus' we are blaming Jesus for our own disobedience. The Bible commands us to care for our families – 1 Timothy 5:8.

6. We don't *earn* the favour of God. That is obviously impossible. Rather, after we have received His free forgiveness in Jesus and

received the righteousness of Jesus, we *are* now willing and able to live *out* what God has worked *in* us. We work hard, study the Bible hard, pray hard, serve hard in order to grow daily more and more like Jesus.

Study 3   Bible Answers

1 Thessalonians 4:1-10

1. The teaching of the Bible is designed to equip and motivate us to live God-pleasing lives, "more and more". To be lazy is to reject the Bible. As we wait on the Living God, He will strengthen us to serve Him. The Day of Jesus is coming... so we must make the most of the short time available. If we are tired or apathetic... call out to Jesus to give us new energy and vision. See Isaiah 40:28-31.

2. If we are set apart as faithful servants of the Holy God, then we must show this in our faithfulness to each other.

3. The heart that has wandered away from the Lord God will also wander away from human commitment and faithfulness. We were made to be utterly faithful to the Lord Jesus... and He also gave us the blessing of experiencing a picture of that as we are utterly faithful to our spouse. Whether we experience this earthly romance or not, yet we are all heading towards the marriage between Jesus and His Church. It is only in Jesus that we find the ultimate relationship we were made for.

4. When Christians are sexually impure – in thoughts and actions – it is an earthly picture of our spiritual adultery. It shows that our hearts are *owned* by another god... pleasure or popularity or excitement.

5. If we genuinely turn from our sin He will forgive and heal us. There is a new beginning and a fresh start beyond anything we can imagine. He doesn't just forgive our sin, but will also set us free from its power. The way of Jesus is to do everything we can to turn from our sin... no matter the cost. This does not mean pretending that it did not happen. If we have betrayed our spouse, we must confess our sin to them. Whatever consequences our sins may have in this passing age, we need to

trust ourselves to Jesus. If we completely follow His way, He can bring good out of our most terrible mess.

6.   Human ways lead to such shame, rejection and abuse. The ways of God lead to dignity, commitment and love. To follow the way of the Living God, who designed us, is always the best. Time usually reveals the truth of this, often more quickly than we imagine. God gives His *Holy* Spirit to support us in His ways of holiness.

7.   God showed us what love is when Jesus gave up everything to die for us. Real love is not about mere words, but self-sacrifice and putting the needs of others ahead of our own.

8.   Love is never finished. We always need more love for each other, to bear with each others weaknesses and needs. There are always new challenges for love.

Study 4   Bible Answers

1 Thessalonians 5:12-18

1. Think of all the challenges of these letters. Think of all we must do and be in order to live worthy lives as we wait for Jesus. It is the job of the church leaders to train and equip us to live these lives. They need respect and love to do this hard work.

2. When we are corrected we should receive that with humility and quietness. Think and pray about what we have been told before speaking to others about our objections, excuses or feelings.

3. The Living God is a loving community. We are the people who are to live out the life of that Living God. Our goal is nothing less than a warm and open love for each other. To merely silently tolerate each other falls very far below the love that God shows to us.

4. The time is short. We can enter into our rest after resurrection morning. Now is the time to 'redeem the time', make the most of the time we have. Think of all the opportunities for service that we have now... that will not be available in the New Creation. Have we won our entire neighbourhood and workplace for Jesus?

5. Leave it to the Lord God. He alone will judge justly. We must trust Him to handle it all as He sees best. Retaliation is a failure to trust the Living God.

6. Satan assumed that Job only served the Lord because he was 'paid' to do it. Satan always assumes that we are all mercenaries at heart.

7. Job focuses on the Living God beyond all possessions and circumstances. Our circumstances come and go, but the Eternal God is the rock that will never change. If we stand on that rock, then we will not be overwhelmed by the changing events of life. Whatever trials the Father allows us to face, He will never abandon us and will always give us the joy and peace we need.

8. How does the fact of Jesus' return affect our daily living? Our use of money? Our use of time? Our career plans? Our hopes for our children?

Study 5   Bible Answers

2 Thessalonians 1:3-10

1. Paul thanks God that the Thessalonians trust Jesus more and more – greater certainty about His way and words, and a greater eagerness to put it into practice. So it is no surprise that this faith is joined with an ever increasing love. The more we trust the way of Jesus, the more we serve one another as He served us.

2. It is not the numbers or money or size that impressed Paul, but the love, faith and perseverance under difficulties.

3. The Thessalonians needed to know that their endurance and faith was praiseworthy and wonderful. The other churches needed to hear about this so that they would be encouraged in their own challenges. The unbelievers who were persecuting the Thessalonians would see that their opposition was not having the effect they intended. Far from destroying the church it was refining it and becoming an opportunity for God's power to be displayed.

4. Jesus showed us how to do this… as do the prophets, apostles and saints of both the Old and New Testaments. If we trust the Living God in all we face we find joy and fruitfulness hidden in the depths of suffering. So many Christians testify that the very best times have been the very darkest times. In our weakness our wonderful God loves to show His mysterious and almighty power.

5. Jesus is not just the cute baby in the manger. Nor is He simply a gentle teacher of peace and tolerance. He is the Living God, the Judge of the Universe, the Master of Death and Hell. When we call to Him we are speaking to the One who can do all things. When we tell others about Him we need to know in our hearts and minds all the glory and majesty, dominion and power, terror and righteousness that the Eternal Lamb of God really is. Rejecting Him is very, very serious.

6.   Knowing God is the same as obeying the gospel of Jesus. We cannot know God unless we have come to Him through Jesus.

7.   Jesus' glory will be revealed *in* us! It is beyond imagination! How can we be caught up and included in that divine glory? It is no wonder we will marvel at one another! If this is what will happen to us, then we should work to show the glory of Jesus within us even now.

Study 6   Bible Answers

2 Thessalonians 3:6-15

1. Idleness is a sign that a person has rejected the teaching of the apostles. It is a very serious matter.

2. How can we recommend the teaching of Jesus and His apostles if we will not live it ourselves? The apostles made sure that they lived in a way that presented the way of Jesus.

3. Paul and his team endured sleepless nights so that they were no burden to the church. They worked as hard as they were able, making enough money to cover all their costs. They were so determined to leave a good example to those new Christians. Do we put in so much effort to give a good example of discipleship in our local churches?

4. We are not saved by trying to be good, but only by the saving death of Jesus. If the message people hear from us concerns moral behaviour issues, then they will conclude that the message of Jesus is to do with 'trying harder to be good'.

5. If the local church is to be the 'showcase' of the teaching of Jesus and His apostles, we have to be very serious if people associate with us yet reject this teaching in word or deed. However, when we deny them a place in the Christian fellowship, we must be motivated by love for them. Our great desire is to restore them into the church.

6. If you knew that Jesus was going to return in one month... what would you do?